SEASONS CHANGE,

LIFE GETS BETTER

Empowering Affirmations for Every Day of the Year

Abby Leigh Hunter

Seasons Change, Life Gets Better

This book is available in multiple formats including Kindle, EPUB e-book, paperback, and hardcover. Print editions are available in Budget (grayscale) and Standard (full-color) editions. Visit the publisher's website at **https://vu.org** for up-to-date details and ISBN numbers for editions currently available. Wholesale orders for print editions may be placed by searching for the desired ISBN in Ingram Content Group's iPage order system.

Inquiries and general correspondence should be addressed to Virtual University Press using the online contact form at **https://vu.org/contact-us/** or direct e-mail inquiries to Editor@VU.org. Our telephone number is (805) 888-0100, and our fax is (805) 888-2999.

ISBN Numbers:

978-1-64399-046-0	Kindle e-book
978-1-64399-045-3	EPUB e-book
978-1-64399-047-7	Budget (grayscale) paperback
978-1-64399-048-4	Standard (full-color) paperback
978-1-64399-049-1	Hardcover (full-color)

Table of Contents

Preface

This book of daily affirmations is a collection of simple but easily forgotten principles of positive thought and living in the moment that can empower you to achieve success and happiness in life. Inspired by the changing seasons, the calendar months and nature's timeless wonder, these passages can serve as reminders that no matter what difficulties you face, when you plant positive seeds, they will blossom into positive results.

Language has always been a powerful catalyst to inspire and motivate, even in the darkest times. A few reassuring words at the right moment can make a tremendous difference in how things turn out. Instead of falling into frustration or despair, you can use these affirmations to reimagine your path forward with confident optimism. It's as easy as taking a few minutes every day to step back from your hectic life, center yourself in the present moment, and reinforce your positive state of mind. Here are some quick and easy ways you can integrate the power of these affirmations into your daily living:

- Pin a quote that resonates with you on your PC or laptop, and change it every few days.

- Write a positive thought on paper and post it near your desk, on your refrigerator, or at another location you where you spend time every day.

- Tape an inspiring note on your bathroom mirror.

- Share your favorite affirmations with friends and family on social media.

- Print out and frame your favorite passages and make them a part of your home décor.

- Keep this book in your backpack at school, in your desk drawer at work, or on a kitchen counter so you can open it for a quick spritz of positivity when your mood falters during the day.

- Text or email a daily message of inspiration to your best friend or others whom you care about.

- Say a favorite passage out loud as a mantra, or write it down to amplify its power as an affirmation.

Seasons change, your life will change, and each year can be better than the last if you take the actions necessary to remain positive and true to your goals. Never lose sight of life's natural order: after every rain comes sunshine; after every storm, a tranquil calm; after night's darkest hours, a new day always dawns bringing new opportunities to fill your life with prosperity and achieve your fondest dreams.

—Abby Leigh Hunter

JANUARY

JANUARY 1

The arrival of a new year brings a mood of reflection and a yearning for something better than the year gone by. It's a time for making resolutions that will bring you closer to your goals. Today is the first page of a new chapter in your life! A new year filled with promise lies ahead: a clean slate, a fresh canvas, ripe with possibility. This year can be anything you want it to be. Your future starts now!

JANUARY 2

View each person you interact with and each challenge you encounter today as an opportunity. They can help you get the year off to a wonderful start—and you can return the favor! Every encounter with a friend, family, or new acquaintance affords a chance for you to make their day a better one. You never know when lending a helping hand or performing a random act of kindness will change someone's life.

JANUARY 3

A typical winter storm drops billions of snowflakes, and each is wonderfully unique. If every positive thought you have is like a snowflake, just imagine the power you have to surround yourself in positive energy and turn your environment into something wonderful.

JANUARY 4

Dwelling on the future can become an obsession that we justify as necessary. Your goals lie in the future, waiting to be accomplished; happiness lurks in the dawn of an elusive tomorrow. Society is future-focused, and you can go nowhere without goals and dreams that hide in the future. Invest the time and energy to lay the groundwork for a successful tomorrow, but don't forget to enjoy today.

JANUARY 5

Many see winter as a time that life goes dormant, trees reach bare limbs to the sky, and flowers lose their bloom. Yet, the brilliant glare of snow on a clear day after a storm makes the sky seem bluer and random splashes of color more vibrant. It's a friendly reminder from nature that even when you are surrounded by snow, a new day can bring warmth, color, and a reminder that spring is never far away.

JANUARY 6

Having been raised in one of the coldest places in North America has taught me that sipping a cup of hot coffee or tea on a frigid January day inspires a deeper appreciation of warmth, even when it expresses in small ways.

JAnuARY 7

Whether today brings stormy weather or a tantalizing glimpse of sunshine, start your morning with positive thoughts, and it could become the best day yet of a promising new year!

JAnuARY 8

The solitude of winter and weeks of harsh weather can make roads impassable and give you lots of time to think. Instead of dwelling on all the things you can't do in the winter, focus on what you can do right now. And once you've done it, you can think about what you'll do in the spring to move your life toward your goals.

JAnuARY 9

The month of January was named after Janus, the Roman god of doorways, gates, and transitions. Janus had two faces and could look back into the past and forward into the future—a metaphor that combines the wisdom of past experience and a clear vision of the future. Use your own past experiences and your vision of what you want in your life to move forward and achieve it.

JAnuARY 10

If you've kept a dream diary, you may have discovered that dreams in the winter are often quite different from summer dreams. A reflection of the subconscious mind, dreams are influenced by your surroundings, including the weather. So it is that your dreams, and the course of your life, is a procession of changing seasons as you navigate through the calendar of your life.

JAnuARY 11

Deep conversations by a fireplace with a special person in your life can dispel the chill of January and make your home warmer. Open communication is essential to make your most cherished relationships grow.

JAnuARY 12

On this twelfth day of the new year, savor every moment of these twenty-four hours. This day will only happen once in your life...how can you make the most of it?

JANUARY 13

In winter's cold embrace, one might often think fondly of bright summer days and romantic moonlit nights kissed by a warm breeze. But after every driving rain and every fierce blizzard, the crisp fresh air of a moonlit winter night brings its own special enchantment.

JANUARY 14

Two weeks into the new year, it's time for a progress check! Are you staying focused on opportunities that lie ahead and maintaining your forward momentum to achieve them? After the festivities and heart-felt resolutions you made on New Year's Eve, there's work to be done! Make sure your new beginnings are on track and that you are charting a course to achieve your goals.

JAnuARY 15

The warming caress of sunshine on your skin on a cold winter day is a pleasure of its own and a certain reminder that even on the coldest, darkest day of the year, warm days and sunshine always lie just ahead.

JAnuARY 16

Every season has its own fashion and accessories. Winter doesn't have to be bleak and cold—it can be fun! Break out your scarves and gloves, your hats, earmuffs, warm socks, and sweaters. Winter, like life, is what you make it!

JAnuARY 17

Martin Luther King Jr. was born on this day in 1929. King was not only a pre-eminent civil rights leader but a reminder of the power of individual action to bring about change. Through Dr. King's tireless work and sacrifices, he proved that one person can make a difference and inspired countless others to join the fight for civil rights and the goal of building a future where all people are treated with dignity and respect.

JAnuARY 18

When you are struggling to stay cool in the sweltering heat of August, you may recall the frosty chill in the air today with whimsical nostalgia. There is much to appreciate in both winter and summer. Find the joy in both, and you will make this year truly wonderful.

JAnuARY 19

If the sun isn't shining today, be your own sunshine and share the light of your positive energy with everyone around you.

JAnuARY 20

A cup of hot cocoa might taste the same in January as it does in July, but there's something about that steaming cup on a frosty winter day that makes it seem a bit warmer and sweeter.

JAnuARY 21

Some days will be good, some easy, others challenging or downright difficult. If you encounter disappointment or an obstacle in your path, turn it into a positive experience—learn from it! Life's most difficult setbacks often hold the greatest opportunities for growth.

JAnuARY 22

Your thoughts have power. They can build a path that leads to blissful happiness or dark despair. Keep positive thoughts in your mind to ensure that you reach a happy destination.

JANUARY 23

A heart filled with love and happiness is the secret to driving out the gloom and cold of a long winter.

JANUARY 24

The deepest snow always melts away, and its water nourishes the earth below, awakening the first colors of spring. The changing seasons can teach us so much about life. Grief always melts away and nourishes compassion. Disappointments fade and become life lessons that help us to reach greater heights. Tears nourish the soul and instill wisdom, compassion, and a greater appreciation for joy.

JANUARY 25

As snow drifts silently from the sky, you might not stop to think that it takes thousands of snowflakes to make a snowball, and millions to kiss the earth with just an inch of snow. Likewise, it takes a great many thoughts and actions to make a successful year, and many years to reach a point where you can look back upon a happy and prosperous life.

JANUARY 26

On this day in 1997, comedian Ellen DeGeneres came out as a lesbian on her television show, *Ellen*. The episode was a groundbreaking moment in LGBTQ+ representation in media. At the time, there were very few openly LGBTQ+ celebrities, and they faced significant discrimination. DeGeneres' coming out publicly had a profound impact on millions of people who were struggling with their own sexuality. Her decision helped to normalize LGBTQ+ identities in popular culture and paved the way for greater acceptance in the years that followed.

JAnuARY 27

Anticipating the first blossoms of spring will make winter's shorter days and colder nights seem less bleak. But spending the coldest weeks of the year yearning for spring won't move you closer to fulfilling your new year's resolutions. Maintain your focus, and remember that one great way to stay warm on the coldest winter day is to move faster!

JAnuARY 28

It may be a frosty winter outside,

but what season is it in your heart?

JAnUARY 29

Find joy in the cold weather, the gathering clouds over-head, the rain sparkling on your windows, the glistening ice and snow on the ground. If you don't, you merely experience less joy while the amount of ice and snow on the ground remains the same.

JAnUARY 30

Taking shelter in your home during a fierce storm, curling up by the fireplace with a great book, and sipping warm tea or rum are simple pleasures that you can only enjoy in the winter.

JAnuARY 31

As January comes to an end, today is a good time to reflect on your accomplishments. Have you spent the thirty-one days in this month grumbling about the winter, or did you make progress laying the groundwork for a productive spring and summer? You are the architect of your destiny. You alone decide the path you walk in life and how far you will go.

FEBRUARY

25

FEBRUARY 1

February is the coldest month of the year in the northern hemisphere, but it's also the month of valentines, flowers, and romance. Love is in the air, and it makes the harsh cold of winter seem warmer and the long, dark nights seem brighter.

FEBRUARY 2

Resolve to do something special today, tomorrow, and every day this month that makes your heart happy.

FeBRuARY 3

The rejuvenating power of nature clears the mind, lightens the heart, and invigorates the soul. Make it a point to go outdoors today, no matter what the weather, and appreciate the vast sky overhead, the silhouette of a lofty tree, the glistening snow, or a bit of green to remind you that the rebirth of spring is never far away.

FeBRuARY 4

Originally called Februarius on the Roman calendar, this month gets its name from the Latin term februum, which means "purification" and coincides with a purification ritual held under the full moon. So, when you gaze up at the night sky and see the glow of the full moon, you might find it inspiring to ponder how many millions of people over the centuries have marveled at the same breathtaking view!

FeBRuARY 5

Wherever you find love,

You will always find life.

FeBRuARY 6

Seasons change and nature's timeless progression from winter to spring to summer and fall reminds us not to fear change. It is natural, inevitable, and a powerful catalyst of growth. Make a plan and follow it; change course when necessary, and you will move closer to your dreams with each passing day.

FEBRUARY 7

Born on this day in 1812, Charles Dickens was a master storyteller who used his talents to bring attention to the struggles and injustices of his time. His writings continue to inspire us to strive for a world where fairness and compassion are the guiding principles. Through his powerful writing and enduring characters, Dickens reminds us of the boundless capacity of the human spirit to overcome even the toughest of circumstances.

FEBRUARY 8

Think of this midwinter day

as a magical arrow you are aiming

at something truly wonderful.

FeBRuaRY 9

All things in life happen for a reason. When you resist disappointment and despair and earnestly search for the underlying reasons, you will gain a deeper understanding of life and a better opportunity to chart your own course and become the master your destiny.

FeBRuaRY 10

Everyone needs a reminder that they are valued and loved. Reach out to someone you haven't talked with for a while and let them know.

FeBRuARY 11

The next time you find yourself grumbling about the cold and dreariness of winter, remind yourself that the rain and snow will be replaced soon enough by ants and mosquitoes.

FeBRuARY 12

Born on this day in 1809, Abraham Lincoln is widely celebrated as one of the most inspiring figures in U.S. history. He is remembered for many memorable speeches and writings, but his most famous was just 272 words long. Delivered shortly after the Battle of Gettysburg, one of the bloodiest battles of the Civil War, the Gettysburg Address is often cited as one of the most inspiring speeches in American history because of its powerful message of unity, sacrifice, and the importance of democracy and freedom. Lincoln concluded the speech with the famous words: "That this nation, under God, shall have a new birth of freedom – and that the government of the people, by the people, for the people, shall not perish from the earth."

FEBRUARY 13

When you love someone deeply, you love who they are and not who you want them to be. Love is accepting. Love is forgiving. Love is infinite. It is impossible to measure how much love the heart can hold.

FEBRUARY 14

Lovers, it's your special day—Happy Valentine's Day! As you celebrate this romantic day, let your heart be filled with love and appreciation for your special someone. May the love you share grow stronger and inspire you to cherish one other, always.

FeBRuARY 15

One of the most significant women in American history was born on this day in 1820. A true inspiration for modern day women (and men!), Susan B. Anthony spent her life advocating equal rights for women, including the right to vote. In a speech she gave at the National Women's Rights Convention in 1856, she argued women must learn to be self-reliant and not depend on men for support: "I declare to you that woman must not depend upon the protection of man, but must be taught to protect herself, and there I take my stand. While I am in favor of the highest possible culture and development of woman, I have yet to find the man, I have yet to find the woman, who is willing to take upon themselves the advocacy of the 'rights' of the women to the extent that they are willing to give to them the 'rights' which they claim for themselves."

FeBRuARY 16

Winter can be many things to many people, and for some, it is a season of darkness and cold. Remember the wise saying that it's always darkest before the dawn, and approach your days this winter as a challenge rather than an obstacle.

FeBRuaRY 17

Although roses are most often associated with February and Valentine's Day, the violet and the primrose are the birth flowers of this month. Violets symbolize patience, loyalty, and fidelity. Give a bouquet of violets to let someone know you will always be there for them. Give a primrose to let your special someone know that you can't live without them.

FeBRuaRY 18

Kindness in your thoughts, words, and actions will keep you warm in even the coldest of months.

FeBRuaRY 19

Fun fact: It takes ten inches of winter snow to equal one inch of springtime rain. Likewise, in our day-to-day affairs, we can accomplish much with minimal effort if we approach challenges in the right way and flow with the tide rather than struggling against it.

FeBRuaRY 20

There are many kinds of love, but the basic need to love and be loved is one constant that unites us all.

FeBRuaRY 21

The coldest day and darkest night of winter will always be followed by the warmest day and star-studded night sky of summer. Seasons change, and if we stay positive and look for the best in every day, our calendar will be filled with happy days and good fortune.

FeBRuaRY 22

The first president of the U.S and hero of the American Revolution, George Washington was born on this day in 1732. Throughout his life, he was a firm believer in the importance of cultivating virtue and inner strength. His writings and speeches frequently stressed the need for individuals to develop good character, to strive for moral excellence, and to cultivate a positive outlook on life. In a letter to his nephew, Bushrod Washington, dated Nov. 10, 1783, he counseled: "Happiness and moral duty are inseparably connected; the latter cannot be attained without the former." These words echo a predominant theme in self-help teachings, old and new, that happiness is a condition we must work toward day by day, and it requires that we strive to develop our own inner being and strength of character.

FeBRuaRY 23

When you stand in the shade on a winter day, it will feel even colder than it is. Move into the light and let it warm you. In day-to-day living, embrace the light and let it warm your soul. Share that light with others, and you'll bring warmth and smiles to everyone around you.

FeBRuaRY 24

Some trees remain green all winter long. They stand strong, enduring the elements and holding snow on their branches until the spring thaw lightens their load. We can learn much from observing how strength and perseverance are rewarded in nature. Seasons change, and life goes on.

FeBRuARY 25

When winter has turned to spring, and spring to summer, you may look back and remember how delightful today actually is when you are sweltering on a ridiculously hot afternoon in August.

FeBRuARY 26

Today is Carpe Diem Day! The Roman poet Horace wrote, "Carpe diem, quam minimum credula postero," which loosely translates to "Seize the day, put very little trust in tomorrow." Other contemporary interpretations are, "Live today like there will be no tomorrow" and "Take nothing for granted." Make your today extraordinary, and encourage your family and friends to do the same.

FEBRUARY 27

Winter teaches perseverance. At just the right moment, the snow begins to melt, dark clouds overhead drift away, and the sun shines through, transforming the world from the icy white of winter to the vibrant colors of spring.

FEBRUARY 28

People have differing views on winter. For some, it's a cold and dreary season. For others, it is a time of peace and wonder. The real beauty is that winter is a little of everything. But almost everyone finds special delight in knowing winter is coming to an end. When the sun rises tomorrow morning, it will be the first day of a magnificent March!

FeBRuARY 29

Every four years, February 29th graces us with its presence, adding an extra day on the calendar—Leap Day. Have you ever wondered why this happens? It's because the earth takes roughly 365.25 days to orbit the sun, and to keep our calendar aligned with the astronomical year, an extra day is added every four years. Leap Day serves as a unique reminder that time is precious. How will you make the most of this gift of an extra 24 hours in your year?

MARCH

MARCH 1

There's an old folk saying that March comes in like a lion, and goes out like a lamb. The month often brings unstable weather in the northern hemisphere as winter turns to spring. The uncertainty of the weather offers a perspective on another wise saying: nothing in life is certain, so everything is possible!

MARCH 2

Find something in nature to enjoy today. The fresh air, the breeze, the random shapes of lazy clouds overhead, all offer something to appreciate in the here and now. Enjoy the moment, and then turn it into a memorable day and a fabulous month.

MArcH 3

Alexander Graham Bell, best known for his invention of the telephone, was born on this day in 1847. He could not have imagined how his device would change the world. When you have a dream, pursue it, but don't overlook opportunities along the way. As Bell once observed: "When one door closes, another door opens; but we so often look so long and so regretfully upon the closed door, we do not see the ones which open for us." This aspirational passage is often interpreted as a call to resilience and optimism in the face of adversity, and two centuries later, it remains a source of inspiration and motivation for many people.

MArcH 4

Approaching life as an adventure requires optimism and courage. You must be willing to try something new, go somewhere you've never gone before, do something you've never done before. Adventures can open doors to new opportunities that you never thought possible. What's keeping you from embarking on an early March adventure? Today is a great day to try something new.

MArcH 5

Today is World Wildlife Day, an annual event introduced by the United Nations in 2013 to raise awareness about the world's endangered species. It reminds us of the threats to wildlife, including habitat loss, poaching, and climate change. This day is a call to action to protect the Earth's biodiversity for future generations.

MArcH 6

As the world awakens from its winter slumber and flowers burst into bloom once again, commit that this Spring season will bring new beginnings, fresh perspectives, and the courage to chase your dreams. Let the rejuvenation of nature inspire you to grow and blossom into the best version of yourself.

MArcH 7

Pause for a few minutes during your day to appreciate nature's wonder as the colors around you change from brown to green, the snows turn to rain, and the sky seems a little bluer, the sun a little warmer.

MArcH 8

Today is International Women's Day. The event has been a global celebration of the social, cultural, and political achievements of women since the early 1900s, and it helps raise awareness about women's rights and equality. What can you do to make a positive difference for women in your community or your country?

MARcH 9

Spring is in the air, and the anticipation is intense; but those who love winter may feel a touch of sadness at the change. Don't let a blue mood detract from the bright blue sky overhead and spring's promise of renewal and new beginnings all around you.

MARcH 10

March weather sometimes feels like winter and summer all wrapped in one day. Whether today brings spring showers, a late winter storm, or a pleasant taste of sunshine, take it in stride. Remember that how you approach the day will determine how the day turns out.

MArcH 11

One of the best ways to feel happier is to let go of the things in your life that don't support that goal. Identify one condition standing in the way of your happiness that you can do something about today—and do it.

MArcH 12

Today is National Plant a Flower Day! It is mainly observed in the United States, but wherever you might be, it's a great time to plant a flower. The symbolism of planting a seed that blossoms with a profuse splash of color and fragrance is unmistakable. Plant a flower in your garden, and watch the joy grow in your heart.

MARcH 13

If March was a perfume, I'd imagine it's a little bit of a cool rain mixed with fragrant spring blossoms, a splash of earthy essence, and deep anticipation.

MARcH 14

Albert Einstein was born on this day in 1879. His theory of relativity revolutionized scientific thought on matter, space and time. Although he never said the popular Internet meme, "The definition of insanity is doing the same thing over and over and expecting different results," Einstein did write: "Imagination is more important than knowledge. Knowledge is limited, whereas imagination embraces the entire world, stimulating progress, giving birth to evolution." He believed imagination was a crucial tool for making new connections, seeing the world in new ways, and generating new ideas. His quote is often interpreted as a call to develop our imagination and creative potential, which are essential for innovation and progress in all areas of human endeavor. Never be afraid to imagine and to dream!

MARCH 15

Today is the Ides of March. Often remembered in history as the day Julius Caesar was assassinated, it has taken on a dark connotation. But the Ides of March was once celebrated as the Roman new year. Imagine—New Year's Day in March! What a great time to recommit yourself to the resolutions you made in January! If your progress has been lagging, resolve to pick up the pace and move forward with your goals.

MARCH 16

Mornings aren't quite as chilly, the daylight hours are growing longer, skies are bluer, and the sun is warmer. Spring is in the air, and if you've taken the time to plant seeds in your spiritual garden, they will soon begin to bloom. Life is a process of cause and effect: send out positive thoughts, and positive things happen.

MARcH 17

Happy St. Patrick's Day! According to Irish folklore, on this day each year, leprechauns hide a pot of gold at the end of a rainbow for you to find. Even if you don't find that rainbow today, you have other blessings to count. Make a list of what you are fortunate to have in your life, and you will realize how truly lucky you are.

MARcH 18

As important as it is for us to learn

from the past and plan for the future,

the key to happiness is

finding the joy in today.

MArcH 19

An unexpected Spring downpour may seem inconvenient at times, but without a little rain, nothing will grow and no rainbows will show.

MArcH 20

The spring (or vernal) equinox often falls on this day, when the sun crosses the equator moving northward and marks the first day of spring in the northern hemisphere. Say goodbye to winter, welcome in the new season, and enjoy your life!

MArcH 21

Today is a remarkable day. It will happen just once in your lifetime. Embrace the day, center yourself in the present moment, and make the most of it.

MArcH 22

If you put out positive energy, that is what you will attract. Happiness creates happiness. Success builds on success.

MArcH 23

Now that spring has returned, those dreary days when you could think of nothing good to say about winter will give you an appreciation for the warm, sunny days to come. As spring bursts into bloom around you, let hope and love blossom in your heart.

MArcH 24

Step outdoors and take a few minutes just for yourself to breathe in the day. Spring is a time of renewal and fresh starts. Inhale the new and exhale the old that no longer inspires or motivates you.

MARCH 25

People change as the days go by. If you are exactly the same person at the end of the day as you were in the morning, your day has been wasted. Learn something new every day. Change an attitude or improve some condition in your life. Strive to be a better person at the end of each day, and your life will be a wonderful adventure.

MARCH 26

Born on this day in 1874, Robert Frost used poetry to explore the complexities of the human experience. He had a deep love for the majesty of nature, reflected in many of his poems. A nonconformist, Frost charted his own course in life and in poetry. He refused to be limited by tradition and conventions, and he followed his own conscience and voice. This courage to be true to himself and his art is a source of inspiration to many.

MARcH 27

The key to success is to accept rejection and failure as a part of the process. It is merely one step in the journey.

MARcH 28

Even the most carefully laid plans don't always ensure success. Accept this as part of life's design and be willing to change course when necessary. There is always more than one path that leads to a goal.

MARcH 29

Do you want to make the world a better place? Make yourself a better person. Don't wait for others to act. Change always begins with you.

MARcH 30

Spring cleaning isn't just about sweeping up dust and discarding junk you no longer want or need. Cleaning is a spiritual exercise; it not only spruces up your living space but refreshes the soul. Life always goes smoother when your thoughts and surroundings are well-organized.

MARcH 31

No doubt you've heard the old proverb, "You reap what you sow." But have you thought seriously about what it means? On the surface, it makes sense: if you plant oats, you won't harvest corn. As spring begins to color the world around you with lush green and fragrant splashes of color, our thoughts may turn to planting flowers and gardens. Thoughts are like seeds. What you plant today is what you will harvest tomorrow.

APRIL

APRIL 1

Today is April Fools' Day, an annual tradition of playing practical jokes observed in many countries of the world. These acts are carried out in a spirit of good fun, and even world leaders and the media have participated in elaborate pranks on this day. If you've decided to join the fun, consider your prank beforehand and make sure those on the receiving end will see the humor in it. As the saying goes, laughter is the best medicine, but that's true only when everyone is laughing about the joke.

APRIL 2

It's a new month, and a gorgeous spring season awaits you. What do you want to accomplish by the end of this month? Don't just think about it—grab your phone, laptop, or a pencil and jot down your goals. Include a few helpful reminders on how you can achieve them. Having a road-map is the surest way to reach your destination.

APrIL 3

Born on this day in 1897, American naturalist and essayist John Burroughs authored many inspiring works on nature and self-improvement, but his most inspiring legacy is the record of his own life. He grew up on a farm and had limited education, but he developed a keen interest in literature and science, and his writings helped shape the environmental movement in the U.S. In addition to his environmental advocacy, Burroughs was committed to personal growth and self-improvement. He believed that everyone has the potential for greatness, and he encouraged people to look within to find their own source of power and inspiration. His writings often explored themes of self-discovery, mindfulness, and the beauty of the natural world, and he remains a beloved figure in American literature and environmental history today.

APrIL 4

Consider the notion of planting your own garden, even a modest one with a sprinkling of flowers. Put some thought into planning it. Life's greatest joys rarely happen by accident.

APrIL 5

Spring reminds us of the beauty in a sudden, approaching storm—tumultuous, unpredictable, and dazzling all in the same breath.

APrIL 6

The warming days of spring and the human emotion we call hope share one common denominator: both are inspired by the promise of good things to come.

APRIL 7

Today is World Health Day, an annual event sponsored by the World Health Organization to advance the truth that "enjoyment of the highest attainable standard of health is one of the fundamental rights of every human being." As the year unfolds, it is imperative that you do everything possible to get healthy and stay healthy. Good health and happiness go hand in hand.

APRIL 8

Buddha (Siddhartha Gautama) was born in Nepal on this day in 563 BCE. Through his teachings, he endeavored to guide others towards enlightenment and liberation from suffering. He once said, as recorded in the *Dhammapada*: "As a bee gathering nectar does not harm or disturb the color and fragrance of the flower, so do the wise move through the world." This teaches us that as a bee collects nectar without harming or disturbing the flower, we should move through the world without causing harm or disruption. The bee and flower exist in a state of interdependence, and by recognizing our own interconnection with the world, we can move through it with awareness, cultivating a sense of inner peace and living in harmony with others.

APRIL 9

As you enjoy the sunny days, the cool clear nights, the gentle April breezes, and the uplifting caress of Sweet Spring, be mindful to build a pathway that will lead you into a joyful summer.

APRIL 10

Cosmetics firms are always trying to bottle the luscious scents of spring into perfumes, but the purest fragrance is free. Step outdoors and take a deep breath of spring air— that can never be put in a bottle, and its value is greater than the world's most expensive perfume.

APrIL 11

A gentle rain is a symphony to the senses and a caress to the soul. Let the sight, sound, and feeling of April showers on your skin inspire a deeper appreciation of nature and how it affects your life from day to day in so many ways.

APrIL 12

If you want to find true happiness, the key is in your thinking. Look beyond the world of material things. Wealth may bring comfort but doesn't ensure happiness. To achieve blissful happiness, it does not matter what you have or don't have; it matters how you think.

APRIL 13

Thomas Jefferson was born on this day in 1743. One of America's Founding Fathers and third president of the U.S., Jefferson was a firm believer in self-empowerment and living by universal principles. In a letter to his friend and colleague, George Wythe, written in 1790, he advised: "Never put off till tomorrow what you can do to-day. Never trouble another for what you can do yourself. Never spend your money before you have it. Never buy what you do not want because it is cheap; it will be dear to you. Pride costs us more than hunger, thirst, and cold. We never repent of having eaten too little. Nothing is troublesome that we do willingly."

APRIL 14

April showers can turn into intense downpours in the northern hemisphere, thanks to the constantly shifting jet stream. But before you wish the rain away, remember that it is an essential part of spring's cycle of renewal. Nothing great can happen in nature without a little rain.

APrIL 15

Leonardo da Vinci was born on this day in 1452. Scientist, painter, sculptor, engineer, architect, and inventor, he designed flying machines and other military devices centuries before they became a reality. His relentless pursuit of knowledge, his innovative spirit, and his ability to think outside the box have inspired millions to pursue their own creative and scientific endeavors. Da Vinci is an immortal reminder that when you have a dream, pursue it—anything is possible!

APrIL 16

"Sweet April showers bring May flowers" is a folk saying handed down to us from the 1500s. It is a reminder that the inconvenience of April's stormy weather is followed by exquisite flowers in May. Likewise, when you are caught up in the turmoil of daily living, take time out to plant seeds in your spiritual garden to bring your hopes and dreams to full bloom.

APrIL 17

Strive to make your world a little better each day. But remember, it's not necessary to make your world perfect. A perfect world is full of imperfections, but that's okay if it's the world you've created and you love being in it.

APrIL 18

An incredible thing about a flower is that it blooms for its own joy and will try its hardest to get to that point no matter where it's planted.

APriL 19

Would spring feel as wonderful if it wasn't for the winter that set the stage for its arrival? The contrast between the two seasons makes spring days seem brighter and more uplifting.

APriL 20

There's something about the magic of April that helps even the saddest hearts feel optimistic about the world outside and tomorrow's possibilities that lie ahead.

APrIL 21

Although January is the customary month for making resolutions and setting goals, why not spring? What better time to re-think your priorities and refocus your energy on your goals than on a beautiful spring day?

APrIL 22

Earth Day is an annual event celebrated on April 22. Sponsored by EarthDay.org, the goal is to protect the environment and bring transformational change to our planet. Their message will have a familiar ring if you have been following these daily readings: you have real power as an individual, and you can make a difference in helping to protect the environment for future generations. To learn more and get involved, browse https://EarthDay.org

APrIL 23

As spring extends into its second month and dark clouds give way to sunshine, April reminds us of all the wonderful reasons to be optimistic and happy. Just look around you.

APrIL 24

Spring comes only once each calendar year, but if you keep it in your heart, it can spring eternal.

APrIL 25

Almost all circumstances tend to meet the expectations they are given. If you think today will be terrible, it will be. If you think today will be fantastic, it will be. You are the driver on the road of life and the creator of your destiny.

APrIL 26

April is an annual reminder from Mother Nature that every cycle of prolific growth is preceded by cold and rainy days.

APrIL 27

The flowers begin to open, the grass begins to thrive, and day by day the clouds turn a little less gray. These subtle changes culminate in a wondrous event that we call the beauty of spring.

APrIL 28

If science ever finds a way to put the glory of spring into a pill, what a magnificent feat that would be. Nature is the best medicine for the soul—it cures almost everything.

APriL 29

One of the happiest thoughts in spring is the knowledge that this wonderful season will come again next year, and the year after. Both in nature and life, there will always be fierce storms of winter followed by the rejuvenating warmth of spring.

APriL 30

Look in the mirror and tell yourself that today is going to be a fantastic day. How do you know? Because you are going to make that happen.

MAY

MAY 1

Spring fever is inspired by the rebirth of nature. You may not even know what it is that your heart so deeply longs for, but you feel it all the same.

MAY 2

As spring bursts into full bloom, its magic infuses new life everywhere and into everything. Look around, and you will see it in places where you've never looked before.

MAY 3

May celebrates and instills the spirit of youth. It tempts you to explore, touch, and experience everything in sight—with no boundaries other than those you impose on yourself.

MAY 4

Spring isn't just a season; it's something you feel with your heart. Nourish it now, cherish it, remember it, carry it with you into the winter months and give it a refresh each new year.

MAY 5

Deep, luscious green is nature's color in May, and no deeper green can be found than that of this month's traditional birthstone, the emerald. This precious and beautiful gemstone is steeped in folklore. According to legend, it attracts love, wealth, power, and a glimpse into the future. Whether you have an emerald or not, spruce up your home and surroundings with the exquisite green hues of nature and make this spring season uplifting and unforgettable.

MAY 6

Mother nature has so much to teach. You need only open your senses and your heart to savor the world around you.

MAY 7

Every year, spring arrives predictably, and sometimes you might take it for granted. But every spring is unique. You watch the same trees and flowers bloom, yet they never bloom in quite the same way as they did the year before.

MAY 8

The eighth of May is Iris Day. Revered around the world for its delicate beauty, this flower gets its name from Greek mythology which honors Iris as the goddess of the rainbow. In Japan, this exquisite flower symbolizes purity and protection from evil. Celebrate the beauty and spirit of spring today by giving an iris to someone you love.

MAY 9

Spring ushers in new beginnings and growth. Just like the flowers that bloom in the sunshine, embrace the good fortune that comes your way and use your own inner strength to bloom into the successful individual you were meant to be. Here's to a season filled with positivity and progress.

MAY 10

Sometimes just marveling at the vibrant blue of the sky and how the clouds drift majestically over the tree tops, you might be inclined to conclude that heaven is here on earth.

MAY 11

Though spring is in bloom all around, not every day may be warm. But there is warmth in each day if you look for it and appreciate it.

MAY 12

Florence Nightingale, "the Lady with the Lamp," was born on this day in 1820. A British nurse and reformer, she is widely regarded as the founder of modern nursing. She believed that two very different groups of people coexist in the world, both necessary to human progress: those satisfied with the status quo and malcontents who yearn for something better. In her book, *Suggestions for Thought* (1870), she wrote: "The progressive world is necessarily divided into two classes—those who take the best of what there is and enjoy it—those who wish for something better and try to create it. Without these two classes, the world would be badly off. They are the very conditions of progress, both the one and the other. Were there none who were discontented with what they have, the world would never reach anything better."

MAY 13

Sometimes you don't realize how deeply you have longed for the spring until you hear the happy chirp of a bird on a bright spring morning.

MAY 14

Even the task of spring cleaning seems a little easier to manage on a mild and beautiful day in May.

MAY 15

Our unique and natural world is a work of art. One of nature's greatest appeals is that anyone can enjoy it free for the asking at any moment of any day.

MAY 16

Another of spring's joyful expressions is the dandelion, especially when it loses its color. Pick one up, make a wish, and blow the petals into the wind.

MAY 17

When you're going through a difficult time, it will help if you remind yourself that seasons change, and life gets better. Sunshine always follows a storm, as surely as one season leads to the next. Your life will change—nothing ever stands still. But if you give it time, the weather always gets better.

MAY 18

Birds always seem happiest in the spring. The frosty cold of winter has yielded to warmth, and the trees where birds make their homes come to life with color.

MAY 19

Whether you realize it or not, you are profoundly influenced by the people with whom you associate and by your surroundings. Surround yourself with love, light, and laughter.

MAY 20

As the days grow longer with the promise of summer on the horizon, enjoy the beauty that each spring morning brings.

MAY 21

There is no better time to be happy than today. Make it a day to remember.

MAY 22

The sun on a bright spring day shines like a beacon of hope, reminding you to bask in the warmth of positivity. Each sun-kissed day offers new opportunities to shed your worries and embrace the joys of life. Let the day inspire and fill you with a renewed sense of purpose and reignite the fire within your soul.

MAY 23

The month of May is bittersweet. We try to hold on to the joy of spring while eagerly anticipating the summer to come.

MAY 24

Your life is the reflection of your daily habits. If that reflection doesn't look the way you want it to, it's time to begin new habits.

MAY 25

"Within man is the soul of the whole; the wise silence; the universal beauty, to which every part and particle is equally related, the eternal ONE. And this deep power in which we exist and whose beatitude is all accessible to us, is not only self-sufficing and perfect in every hour, but the act of seeing and the thing seen, the seer and the spectacle, the subject and the object, are one. We see the world piece by piece, as the sun, the moon, the animal, the tree; but the whole, of which these are shining parts, is the soul."

The Over-Soul
—Ralph Waldo Emerson
born on this day in 1820

MAY 26

Summer is fast approaching—you can feel it in the air! The days are growing longer and the nights are alive with a special energy.

MAY 27

Sometimes change is inconvenient. But change is necessary. It motivates you to push on through life and brings you closer to your goals. Some of those goals may not be what you envisioned, but they will bring much greater rewards.

MAY 28

As spring unfolds around you and the days grow longer, you might wonder: is one season any more beautiful than the next? In truth, every season brings its own special charm. Endeavor to make every season in your life better than the one before, and you'll be abundantly blessed with success and happiness.

MAY 29

There's nothing like the smell of fresh-cut grass to remind you that a lawn keeps growing no matter how many times you cut it down.

MAY 30

As May comes to an end, the sweet scents of Spring mix into the tantalizing whims of June.

MAY 31

"This is what you shall do: love the earth and sun and the animals, despise riches, give alms to everyone that asks, stand up for the stupid and crazy, devote your income and labor to others, hate tyrants, argue not concerning God, have patience and indulgence toward the people, take off your hat to nothing known or unknown or to any man or number of men, go freely with powerful uneducated persons and with the young and with the mothers of families, read these leaves in the open air every season of every year of your life."

Leaves of Grass
—Walt Whitman
born on this day in 1819

JUNE

JunE 1

Welcome to June and the next wonderful day in your life! With blue skies overhead and flowers in bloom all around, Mother Nature gives a wonderful reminder that no matter what is going on in your daily affairs, sometimes a little bit of sunshine is all you need.

JunE 2

Life is the ultimate teacher. Things may not always go as planned, but you can learn valuable lessons from the events and experiences of today.

JunE 3

Few things are as effective as a bright June day to put you in a sunny disposition. A picnic, a walk in the park or on the beach, or just getting out and walking the dog are a few of the many ways that you can make today productive and perhaps even unforgettable.

JunE 4

Living on the scenic California coast, I've experienced what the locals called "June gloom." The term refers to the fog that often rolls in from the ocean at this time of year. It can seem a bit gloomy because the fog hides the sun, but it keeps the weather delightful and provides a reminder that even gloomy days have a purpose.

JunE 5

Today is World Environment Day, an annual event sponsored by the United Nations to bring attention to the environmental crises our planet faces, from global warming to wildlife extinction, overpopulation, and ocean pollution. "We cannot turn back time. But we can grow trees, green our cities, rewild our gardens, change our diets, and clean up rivers and coasts. Our generation can make peace with nature." Learn more about how you can help protect earth's fragile environment at:
https://WorldEnvironmentDay.global

JunE 6

The delicious scent of rain, flowers, and fresh-cut grass can get you through even the dreariest days.

JunE 7

June is synonymous with joyous, jubilant, jovial, and just plain enjoyable. If you didn't enjoy your first week of the month, hit the reset button. Change your attitude or perspective, and you'll make next week better!

JunE 8

Your garden may not look like your neighbor's, but you both can find the same amount of joy there.

JunE 9

If there is a such thing as a perfect day, it is certainly in June. Remember this pleasant sunny day when you are wrapping up in a heavy coat and gloves and scraping ice off your car windshield this winter.

JunE 10

Sunshine is like a golden smile sprinkled over everything from the lush green grass underfoot to the distant hills. It's a warm greeting from Mother Nature.

JunE 11

As the days grow longer giving you more time to bask in the light, make the most of each day, and be happy.

JunE 12

When you are imagining your future as you would like it to be, reach for the stars and imagine something fantastic. Then, remember the liberating words of the great Spanish painter Pablo Picasso:

"Everything you can imagine is real."

In this simple yet profound advice, Picasso is encouraging us to embrace our imagination and to see it as a tool for creating and manifesting our own reality. This is one of Picasso's most enduring quotes and has resonated with creatives around the world who share his passion for exploring the possibilities of the human imagination.

JunE 13

Today is Weed Your Garden Day, an event that encourages all who garden to pull up the noxious weeds that zap nutrients from the soil and create unsightly growth. Spend a half—hour weeding your garden, and as you do, give some thought to doing the same in your spiritual garden. Remove the unwanted conditions that zap your vitality and distract you from pursuing your highest ambitions.

JunE 14

Some scenes in nature are timeless, and the words used to describe them ring true no matter how long ago they were written. A century ago, in 1926, Canadian author Lucy Maud Montgomery perfectly captured the mood of a romantic summer night in her novel, *The Blue Castle:* "She did not ask to be loved. It was rapture enough just to sit there beside him in silence, alone in the summer night in the white splendor of moonshine, with the wind blowing down on them out of the pine woods." Through the journey of her heroine, Montgomery explores the timeless themes of self-discovery, freedom, and the power of love to transform one's life. Her classic is worth reading for its memorable characters, lush descriptions of nature, and a message of hope and optimism in the face of adversity.

JunE 15

All it takes is a hand to hold on a moonlit June night to reveal the true meaning of summer love.

JunE 16

Every day is a new beginning. Take a deep breath and make today into whatever you want it to be.

JunE 17

With spring in retreat and the summer solstice less than a week away, Mother Nature provides an enduring reminder that life is a cycle. Seasons change, life refreshes and begins anew.

JunE 18

A gentle breeze wafting through the trees on a mild June day can calm even the deepest worries and fears.

JunE 19

Today is Juneteenth, a U.S. holiday that celebrates the end of slavery in America. It is observed in many parts of the world to celebrate African-American culture. Juneteenth was observed for the first time in 1866, when slaves in Texas first learned of the Emancipation Proclamation that set them free, which had been signed by Pres. Abraham Lincoln more than two years earlier.

JunE 20

On this day in 1969, Apollo 11 landed on the moon. As astronaut Neil Armstrong stepped onto the rocky lunar surface, he spoke a phrase that would be immortalized in human history: "That's one small step for man, one giant leap for mankind." Tonight, as you gaze up at the moon and stars, you may realize that each day of your life is one small step in a remarkable journey to your destiny.

JunE 21

The June solstice marks the first day of summer in the northern hemisphere and the longest day of sunlight in the year. The solstice falls on the 20th or 21st of June, depending on when the sun reaches its highest and northernmost point in the sky. In 2022 and 2023, the summer solstice occurs on June 21; in 2024 and 2025, it falls on the 20th. Those who love summer wait all year for this magic moment. Enjoy the season, and make it the best summer of your life!

JunE 22

Though the fresh aroma of spring

brings violets and lavender,

the bright, sunny days of summer

bring the sweet fragrance of roses.

JunE 23

In his novel *The Great Gatsby,* F. Scott Fitzgerald reminds us of the sense of renewal and possibility that comes with the start of a new season, especially summer. The book's fictional narrator Nick Carraway remarks: "And so with the sunshine and great bursts of leaves growing on the trees, just as things grow in fast movies, I had that familiar conviction that life was beginning over again with the summer." The imagery conveys a sense of vitality and growth, as everything comes alive again after a long winter. But as the story unfolds, the beauty and excitement of this world proves fragile and fleeting, subject to the whims of fate and human desire. So while we should proceed enthusiastically and make the most of the summer, we also need a sensible plan built on realistic expectations of what we can actually accomplish.

JunE 24

One afternoon in late June, I went for a walk with my fiancé. It was a beautiful day, and we'd been looking forward to our walk since early that morning. As we made our way up a scenic trail, dark clouds rolled in, and it began to rain. We were disappointed, even a bit annoyed; but then the rain stopped as quickly as it had begun. We found ourselves gazing up at not one but two gorgeous rainbows. It was nature's reminder to both of us that you cannot enjoy rainbows without a little rain.

JunE 25

Glorious summer sunsets rekindle the spark of youth that slumbers in your soul. Don't get so caught up in the challenges of daily living that you miss out on opportunities to enjoy the little things in life that matter the most.

JunE 26

If you could save June in a bottle, just think of the light it would give off on a cold, bleak day in January.

JunE 27

Born on this day in 1880, Helen Keller was a social activist, writer, and an inspiration for millions of people with disabilities. Despite being left deaf and blind from an illness at a young age, Keller overcame impossible odds, and with the help of a teacher, she learned to read, write, and speak, even though she could not see or hear. Her perseverance and determination in learning these skills are a testament to the power of the human spirit. So, the next time you find yourself facing obstacles and adversity, remember that if Helen Keller could turn lemons into lemonade and carve out a place for herself in history, know that you can succeed and reach your heart's desires.

JunE 28

Writer, philosopher, and composer Jean-Jacques Rousseau was born on this day in 1712. A strong advocate for democracy and people having a say in their government. He believed in the importance of freedom and the natural goodness of human beings. His writings are proof that positivity has been part of the human equation since the dawn of civilization. Let positivity be your guiding light today and forward as you bask in the light of sunny days and summer nights.

JunE 29

Every day, you have a choice in deciding how you want to live. You can be happy or sad. You can be angry or at peace. The choice is always yours.

JunE 30

With mild weather and blue skies to delight the senses, what an inspiring way to close out the first half of the year. Take a break from routine, do something fun or relaxing, and pat yourself on the back for the progress you've made so far to fulfill your new year's resolutions.

JULY 1

July brings the promise of warm summer days and starry nights. Let the nourishing sunshine heal your body and the magical evenings heal your soul. If you look up into the sky at just the right moment tonight, you might see a shooting star. Make a summer wish, and then act to make your wish come true!

JULY 2

Every day of your life should be special, but today is unique: it's the 183rd day of the calendar year, which means the second half of the year begins now! How are your New Year's resolutions progressing? Get motivated, and move forward!

JuLY 3

If you always believe something wonderful is about to happen, it always will. And if you don't get exactly what you want exactly when you want it, go with the flow and you will always sail into something even better.

JuLY 4

The Fourth of July is celebrated in America with fireworks, parades, picnics, and parties to commemorate the signing of the Declaration of Independence on this day in 1776. If you observe this holiday, remember that freedom can take many forms. One of the most important is free will—the freedom to think as you wish, to choose your path in life, and to be the maker of your own destiny.

JuLY 5

"When a person opposes or hinders the expression of a great ideal, and is unwilling to believe that he will meet his fellow men as soon as he has penetrated deeply enough into every soul, he is preventing himself from realizing the unlimited. All beliefs are simply degrees of clearness of vision. All are part of one ocean of truth. The more this is realized the easier is it to see the true relationship between all beliefs, and the wider does the vision of the one great ocean become."

The Art of Being and Becoming
Inayat Khan
born on this day in 1882

JuLY 6

The days are long, the sun is bright, and the nights are warm and magical. What more could anyone ask for in a month?

JULY 7

On a day that you are struggling to overcome disappointment or adversity, or if you're just having a hard time staying positive, do not lose sight of the fact that today is but one small step in your soul's eternal journey. A lifetime of wonderful days lies ahead.

JULY 8

A picnic on a quiet July afternoon is a great way to set your heart at ease. It's even better when you share the day with a best friend or someone you love.

JULY 9

Freedom of choice and free will are the most important tools you have for building a happy and prosperous future. Use them to make every day of your life better than the last.

JULY 10

See all that bright sunshine out there? It's yours. What can you do with it to make the rest of your day perfect?

JuLY 11

Remember this sage advice—no words could be truer: success doesn't come from what you do occasionally; it comes from the positive actions you turn into habits.

JuLY 12

"It is a momentous fact that a man may be good, or he may be bad; his life may be true, or it may be false; it may be either a shame or a glory to him. The good man builds himself up; the bad man destroys himself. But whatever we do we must do confidently (if we are timid, let us, then, act timidly), not expecting more light, but having light enough. If we confidently expect more, let us wait for it."

Life Without Principle
Henry David Thoreau
born on this day in 1817

JuLY 13

It's tempting to kick back and daydream about the past, but don't live in it or dwell on memories. Right now, the present requires your attention, and tomorrow's infinite possibilities are swirling around just ahead. Keep moving forward in the calendar, not back.

JuLY 14

You can be in a bad mood, but there are no bad days this month—or ever—unless you choose to let them happen.

JuLY 15

Summer music, summer love, summer food—nothing creates a brighter smile or a happier spirit than the joy of living in the here and now on a glorious day in July.

JuLY 16

You may not know where you are going on the road of life, but you are on your way. Today is a perfect day to do something positive and take a courageous step in your life journey.

JULY 17

Spend a little quiet time outdoors

on a warm July night,

and you will never see

the stars shine so bright.

JULY 18

A wise friend and editor once told me that there's an incredible story worth writing in every summer. What story will you write today?

JuLY 19

Summer days, golden and glowing.

Laughter and happiness,

growing and flowing.

JuLY 20

When you face the sun and move forward confidently into your day, all your worries will vanish into the shadows behind you.

JULY 21

If you love the sunny days and romantic nights of summer, remember that it's always summer somewhere in the world. Hold it inside your heart and you can enjoy this wonderful season every day of the year.

JULY 22

Every cell in the human body replaces itself over the span of seven years. And during those seven years, if you put forth the effort, you will learn more about life's mysteries and grow into a better version of yourself. In nature's eternal, intricate plan, as the seasons change, so do we.

JuLY 23

A brisk walk on a clear July morning is a sure way to energize the body and brighten the soul.

JuLY 24

Lemonade may be refreshing in the fall, but there's nothing like an iced lemonade on a hot summer day to bring a smile to one's face.

JULY 25

Sunsets in every season are beautiful, but those in July seem to glow the brightest, making them spectacular. Take the time to enjoy a summer sunset, and you will be reminded that life's simplest pleasures are often the best.

JULY 26

Irish playwright and political activist George Bernard Shaw was born on this day in 1856. An advocate for social and political reform, his views on women's rights, war, and socialism often sparked debate. In his 1902 play, Mrs. Warren's Profession, Shaw expressed a key principle echoed by many self-help gurus today: "People are always blaming circumstances for what they are. I don't believe in circumstances. The people who get on in this world are the people who get up and look for the circumstances they want, and, if they can't find them, make them." The takeaway is that we are free to pursue their own goals and aspirations, but we also have a duty to use our talents and resources for the betterment of society as a whole.

JULY 27

Summer memories can last a lifetime and keep you warm in the darkest of times.

JULY 28

You want summer to hurry up and arrive, but then go by slowly while it's here. It's the kind of conundrum that might leave you wishing that you were the boss of time itself.

JULY 29

Summer is more than a season. It's a warm and wonderful state of mind that you can enjoy anywhere and anytime.

JULY 30

Born on this day in 1863, Henry Ford was a firm believer in the saying, "The more you give, the more you receive." The wealthy industrialist gave generously to many social causes and believed in using his wealth to make the world a better place for everyone. Interestingly, the more he gave, the wealthier he became, and the more had had to give. Therein lies an important lesson about giving that's worth remembering in day-to-day living.

JuLY 31

If you dream big but sometimes get discouraged, the life story of Catherine Cookson proves that everything is possible. Born out of wedlock to an alcoholic mother and bigamist father, she dropped out of school at fourteen and labored for a decade as a domestic servant. She married, had four miscarriages caused by a rare disease, and fell into depression that led to a mental breakdown. She took up writing as therapy to cope with her depression—and found her life's calling. She went on to write nearly 100 books and sell over 120 million copies in 20 languages. Obstacles and setbacks in life are inevitable, and being knocked down is part of the process of growing stronger. But never give up or accept defeat. You are the architect of your destiny, and you can rise as high as you dare to dream.

AUGUST

AUGUST 1

August is the mid-point in the summer season, so there's plenty more sunshine to enjoy. But regardless of the season, take a few minutes to appreciate and make the most of each uniquely wonderful day.

AUGUST 2

What's special about a strawberry? It allows you to hold all the sweetness and joy of summer in the palm of your hand.

AUGUST 3

When you look back over the years, don't be surprised if your fondest memories are made from June, July, and August. What wonderful memories will you make this summer?

AUGUST 4

There's something remarkably special about a warm August night on the porch, chatting with someone you love by the soft glow of a candle or under a full moon. When you find your place in the universe, you will know where you belong.

AUGUST 5

When your day takes an unexpected turn that puts you on the edge of losing your patience, inhale deeply and remind yourself that the only bad days in August are the ones you choose not to enjoy.

AUGUST 6

Every sunrise in August, and every sunset in this month of midsummer night dreams, is different. All are beautiful and unique.

AUGUST 7

Life, like the four seasons, is a constantly unfolding story of transition. The end of one chapter always takes you to the beginning of the next.

AUGUST 8

The shimmering green peridot is the gemstone of August. Similar in appearance to an emerald, it was called it the "sun gem" by the ancient Egyptians, who believed it could be used to harness the power of nature. Down through the centuries, in Polynesia and Europe, peridot beads have been worn to ward off evil and attract happiness, love, and riches. Give a peridot ring or necklace to your favorite person to help attract good fortune, or wear the gemstone yourself to brighten up your life.

AUGUST 9

Put aside your worries and start your day with a calm, deep breath, and this affirmation: It's great to be alive!

AUGUST 10

The hot, gusty winds of August can stir the restless soul. It's time for something amazing to happen today...but what?

AUGUST 11

"All in all, it was a never-to-be-forgotten summer—one of those summers which come seldom into any life, but leave a rich heritage of beautiful memories in their going—one of those summers which, in a fortunate combination of delightful weather, delightful friends and delightful doing, come as near to perfection as anything can come in this world."

Anne's House of Dreams
Lucy Maud Montgomery

AUGUST 12

Rain or shine, cloudy or bright, uncomfortably hot or pleasantly cool, summer is a state of mind. It's up to you to fill the season with positive days and memories that will last for a lifetime.

AUGUST 13

Sometimes all you need is

a quiet corner in a summer garden

to truly find yourself.

AUGUST 14

Even though summer tans will fade away, you can keep the warmth of these days with you always. Cherish the memories and build on them for a lifetime of happy tomorrows.

AUGUST 15

The greens in nature are most vibrant in summer, the soil the richest, the sky its bluest; and some days, when the sun is high overhead and the air is clear, it seems like you can reach up and touch the clouds. What a perfect time to dream.

AUGUST 16

On the next clear evening, go outdoors for a walk. Gaze up at the stars and marvel for a moment at how vast the universe is and what incredible mysteries await discovery beyond our mundane world. Then, realize how fortunate you are to be alive and a part of this incredible cosmic wonder.

AUGUST 17

We often spend our time worrying about what tomorrow might bring, but as Dale Carnegie once quipped, today is the very tomorrow we worried about yesterday. Instead of getting caught up in the worries and distractions of today, focus on making the most of these twenty-four hours. Be mindful of lessons learned in the from the past but stay focused on the present and take action now to create the bright future you desire. Remember, every moment is an opportunity to shape your destiny!

AUGUST 18

Of the four seasons, summer is most often seen as a time for carefree adventure. You can dance on the grass. Dance in the sun. Dance in the rain. No matter what today brings, enjoy it, and know that tomorrow will be another beautiful day.

AUGUST 19

Today is World Humanitarian Day, a global event sponsored by the United Nations to honor humanitarian and healthcare workers around the world who have been killed or injured while helping others. These unsung heroes gave their lives to make the world a better place. This day keeps their memory alive in the hearts of friends, loved ones, and strangers.

AUGUST 20

H.P. Lovecraft was born on this day in 1890. A master of horror fiction, his legacy captivates readers with his unique writing style and vivid imagination. His stories are a testament to the boundless potential of the human mind, teaching us to push beyond our self-imposed limitations and to be open to new possibilities that may exist beyond our limited senses. Let Lovecraft's ability to conjure up new worlds and imagine the unimaginable inspire us to have the courage to explore and embrace the unknown in our own lives.

AUGUST 21

Do something special today and create a happy memory that will endure through the summer and make you smile for the rest of your life.

AUGUST 22

Science fiction great Ray Bradbury was born on this day in 1920. He began writing short stories at the age of 12, and although his formal education ended when he graduated from high school, he followed his dream of being a writer. He published his first story at age 23 and went on to achieve world renown through his writing. In 1999, he suffered a stroke but fought his way back to recovery and wrote a new novel in 2001. Some people know what they want to do in life and they do it. DO you know what you want to do? Move forward and achieve it!

AUGUST 23

If you planted a garden this year, you saw firsthand proof that "You reap what you sow." You can't expect to harvest sweet corn if you plant bitter herbs. Likewise, you can't expect to attract happiness and prosperity into your life if you don't plant the right seeds. Your actions create reactions that will bring your hopes and dreams to fruition or lead to disappointment. What you plant in your spiritual garden, and the time you spend weeding it, most definitely matter.

AUGUST 24

You must expect to encounter obstacles on the path you are traveling. They are inevitable. But for every obstacle you encounter, there is always a way around it.

AUGUST 25

Russian writer and philosopher Leo Tolstoy was born on this day in 1890. He is regarded as one of the greatest novelists in history, and his epic works include *War and Peace* and *Anna Karenina.* In one passage from his book, *Three Methods of Reform,* Tolstoy stresses the importance of personal responsibility in creating positive change in the world, and his words can serve as a guiding light in our day-to-day living: "There can be only one permanent revolution—a moral one; the regeneration of the inner man. How is this revolution to take place? Nobody knows how it will take place in humanity, but every man feels it clearly in himself. And yet in our world everybody thinks of changing humanity, and nobody thinks of changing himself."

AUGUST 26

While many people were focused on COVID-19 during the summer of 2020, August 26 of that year was an important date in the struggle for women's rights. It was the 100-year commemoration of the ratification of the Nineteenth Amendment to the U.S. Constitution, which gave women the right to vote. Today is our chance to thank to the millions of women who struggled over the years to make our society freer and more enlightened.

AUGUST 27

Surround yourself with happiness and motivation. There is no better time to do that than right now.

AUGUST 28

During this magnificent month of August, there will come a day when the splendor of summer melts with subtle perfection into the crisp fall air.

AUGUST 29

In the waning days of summer, we yearn to hold on just a little longer to sunshine, blue skies, amazing sunsets, and bright memories we'll never forget. Make one of those happy, unforgettable memories today.

AUGUST 30

The Endless Summer is a movie from the 1960s about two surfers who travel the world in search of the perfect wave. But it's not just a film about surfing; it's a story about being young, free, and filled with the spirit of adventure. Every day of your life can be an endless summer if you approach life with the right attitude.

AUGUST 31

To recognize an approaching change in the seasons is to be aware. To be aware is to be alive. Being alive means that you have the power to choose your course and make your life what you want it to be.

SEPTEMBER

SePTeMBeR 1

It's the first day of autumn on our modern calendar, although the seasonal change is often associated with the autumn equinox later this month. Either way, enjoy the final taste of summer's sweetness and begin making plans for the transition to fall.

SePTeMBeR 2

No doubt you've heard the adage, "Make every day count!" Imagine being a citizen of Britain or its colonies and going to sleep on September 2, 1752—but when you wake up the next day, it is September 14. It happened! Riots erupted because people believed the government had cheated them out of eleven days, and they demanded those days back. The "lost" days occurred when Britain adopted the Gregorian calendar and had to adjust for past leap years. Adding more confusion, New Year's Day was moved from March 21 to January 1! Fortunately, our modern calendar is quite reliable, so you can make the most of all 365 days in this year!

153

SePTeMBeR 3

Be thankful for the lessons in your past, and use them to build your future.

SePTeMBeR 4

As the first leaves of autumn turn golden and begin to fall, remember all the joys and festivities for which the coming season is beloved.

SePTeMBeR 5

Pessimists believe individuals can't make a difference in our world unless they are incredibly rich. Not true! Edward Appleton, born on this day in 1892, made a discovery that went unappreciated for a century, but it eventually made wireless communication possible and gave us technology we now take for granted, including wi-fi computing and smartphones. You can make a difference —you may even change the world! You have to believe in yourself, and you have to make the effort.

SePTeMBeR 6

What a wonderful opportunity September brings. You can make this month into whatever you want it to be.

SepTemBeR 7

As summer retreats and the nature whispers the first hints of autumn, the changing season should never be a cause for regret. Fall brings cooler weather, a fresh mindset, and new opportunities to advance your plans and reach your goals. While flowers fade, we reap from the harvest.

SepTemBeR 8

International Literacy Day was introduced in 1967, when UNESCO proclaimed the global importance of literacy. An estimated 773 million adults around the world cannot read or write, and most will suffer a life of hardship and poverty. Many of us take literacy for granted, along with the many other privileges we enjoy in daily life. The next time you're feeling down, be thankful that you are walking in your shoes and able to read this book!

SepTeMBeR 9

How wonderful the cool autumn air is when you mix it with the warmth of sunshine kissing your face.

SepTeMBeR 10

There is more gold in autumn than all the other seasons combined. Fall sunsets compliment the season in such a wonderful way with vibrant shades of crimson, maroon, and orange painting each breathtaking sunset a little different than the last. How many sunsets will you enjoy this month?

SePTeMBeR 11

Fall days are a mix of spring, summer, and winter rolled into a magnificent summer finale and a prelude to golden leaves and cooler weather.

SePTeMBeR 12

It's natural to embrace the happy memories of summer on the one hand, and to anticipate the winter holidays on the other—but the best thing you can do on this glorious fall day is enjoy the weather and turn today into a golden opportunity.

SePTeMBeR 13

In 2003, life coach Dr. Kirsten Harrell proposed that Sept 13 should be recognized as Positive Thinking Day, and it is now a worldwide event. Harrell had been dealing with chronic pain, made worse by surgery, and as she explored alternative healing systems, she realized the power of the mind-body connection and its effect on health. Science has proven that positivity can help heal body, mind, and soul. Celebrate today by writing a positive affirmation, and let it guide your thoughts to a wonderful, inspiring place.

SePTeMBeR 14

When you see the colorful swirls of leaves

creating random patterns on the ground

or dancing in a sudden gust of wind,

that's when you know autumn is in the air.

SepTemBeR 15

So often we fear change, and we try to avoid it at every turn. Progress requires change. Without it, we become stagnant and our affairs bog down in inertia. Welcome change and find the ways to benefit from it.

SepTemBeR 16

Trees demand your attention now as they put on a dazzling show of Mother Nature's artistry, showcasing a rustic pallet sprinkled with nature's gold. Prepare for a magnificent autumn display in the days ahead.

SePTeMBeR 17

Today is the perfect mid-September day to move forward and get one step closer to your dreams.

SePTeMBeR 18

One last evening by a campfire with family, friends, or someone special is a great way to welcome autumn. Add in some enjoyable conversation, let the dancing flames warm your soul, and enjoy being in this moment.

SePTeMBeR 19

Never fear disappointment. Embrace it as a reason to grow more determined. Accept failure as merely a brief stopover on the journey to success. Mistakes lead to correction and progress.

SePTeMBeR 20

For the fashion-conscious, fall can be so much fun. Hats, boots, gloves, and scarves with vibrant patterns and the latest trendy colors can accentuate the season. Boost your self-esteem with a new outfit, and embrace a positive outlook to imagine the possibilities this new season will bring.

SepTeMBeR 21

British author H.G. Wells was born on this day in 1866. Writing in his book, *The Discovery of the Future*, he observed: "The past is but the beginning of a beginning, and all that is or has been is but the twilight of the dawn." The passage holds a powerful message, suggesting that what has happened is only the beginning of what is to come, and the future holds limitless potential beyond what we've already experienced. The metaphor of the "twilight of the dawn" suggests that the past is just the dim, fading light of what is to come. Progress and endless possibilities lie ahead, and we must look to the future rather than dwelling on the past.

SepTeMBeR 22

The autumnal equinox is an astronomical event that marks the arrival of fall, when the sun crosses the equator from north to south and the hours of daylight and darkness are nearly equal across the planet. The fall equinox occurs on Sept. 22 in 2021, 2022, 2024, and 2025; and on Sept. 23 in 2023. The arrival of fall signals that the year is winding down. The goals you've set out to accomplish should be well within sight.

SePTeMBeR 23

The bountiful harvest that happens every fall is a timeless reminder of what all the other seasons are for.

SePTeMBeR 24

"In my younger and more vulnerable years my father gave me some advice that I've been turning over in my mind ever since: 'Whenever you feel like criticizing any one,' he told me, 'Just remember that all the people in this world haven't had the advantages that you've had.'"

The Great Gatsby
F. Scott Fitzgerald
born on this day in 1896

SepTeMBeR 25

As leaves begin to fall and the air turns crisp, embrace the change. Fall is a reminder that life is constantly evolving. Almost every day, it will present new opportunities for renewal and positivity. Walk boldly forward into this season with a mindset of growth and hope.

SepTeMBeR 26

Breathe in the crisp fall air, hold your head high, and keep your mind focused on the goals you want to accomplish as glorious autumn begins to unfold.

SePTeMBeR 27

Autumn leaves are nature's gold, a precious currency as old as time itself and a reassurance, once each year, that no matter how chaotic our human affairs may be, life goes on.

SePTeMBeR 28

As seasons change, embrace the change! Every day of your life can be special, and every day gives you a new chance to move closer to your dreams.

SePTeMBeR 29

When you hear other people criticize you, doubt your abilities, or predict that you cannot succeed, double your efforts. Walk faster, move forward, and leave their negativity far behind.

SePTeMBeR 30

On a wonderful, cool evening when the sun has dipped below the horizon in a kaleidoscope of golden colors and the bright harvest moon drifts overhead, that's when you know that summer has turned into autumn.

OCTOBER

OCTOBER 1

Welcome to October! Only ninety-one days remain in the year. Take stock of which new year's resolutions you've accomplished this year, and which goals remain. Start every day with a definite plan to move forward toward the goals you haven't yet realized, and make each day count.

OCTOBER 2

Born today in 1869, Mahatma Gandhi devoted his life to the cause of Indian independence from British rule. His philosophy of nonviolent resistance, called Satyagraha, influenced civil rights and freedom movements around the world. Gandhi believed in the power of peaceful protest, and he united millions of people from diverse backgrounds in the fight against oppression. His message of love, compassion, and the importance of living a simple life has also inspired many to strive for a better world. When bad days convince us that a better world will never happen, his words remind us otherwise: "You must not lose faith in humanity. Humanity is an ocean; if a few drops of the ocean are dirty, the ocean does not become dirty."

OcTOBeR 3

October is the tenth month in the Gregorian calendar, but in old Rome, it was the eighth month ("octo" from Latin means "eight"). The birthstone of this month is opal, a gem long associated with purity, truth, and hope. The early Greeks believed opals bestowed the gift of prophecy— however, a glimpse of the future only reveals tomorrow's possibilities. You are the architect of your destiny, and your future will be built on the choices you make and the actions you take in the here and now.

OcTOBeR 4

On this day in 1957, Russia launched the first satellite, Sputnik I, into orbit, and it sent a radio signal back to earth for 21 days. This historic event prompted the U.S. to invest heavily in being the first to land on the moon. This required NASA to develop new inventions and technologies that yielded huge benefits for mankind and changed our world. Sometimes the benefits that you encounter on the way to your goal are more important than the goal itself.

OCTOBER 5

Robert Goddard, widely considered the Father of the Space Age, was born on this day in 1882. Despite public ridicule, he devoted his life to the dream of building a machine capable of flying into space. In 1926, he launched the first liquid-fueled rocket from a farm in rural Massachusetts. In 1935, his rocket broke the sound barrier. He also invented a rocket guidance system and self-cooling rocket engine. Never give up on your dreams, and when others doubt that you can succeed, let it strengthen your resolve to prove them wrong.

OCTOBER 6

Celebrate the cooler fall weather with an inspiring sunset walk. Bring along a partner or spend some quality "alone time" enjoying nature's glory.

OcToBeR 7

October brings sweet anticipation for the delicious smell of pumpkins, spices, apple cider, and the winter festivities to come. Instead of dreading the holidays, start making plans to make this year's holiday season the happiest ever.

OcToBeR 8

Today has the same number of hours, minutes, and seconds as yesterday. Tomorrow will be the same. Endeavor to make each day one more step in a journey that brings you closer to your dreams.

OCTOBER 9

As trees release their golden leaves, it is nature's way of freeing them from the weight they bear in the summer and preparing for winter's sleep. It's refreshing to let things go.

OCTOBER 10

October brings opportunities for a multitude of enjoyable activities. Make a list of places you want to go and things you want to do. Then, make time to create happy memories to warm your soul through the winter and into the new year.

OCTOBER 11

October is the time for sweaters and gloves, pumpkins galore, and the rich aroma of caramel-dipped apples. A special energy is in the air that happens only in the fall. Mornings turn brisk and evenings bring golden sunsets. What a wonderful world we live in!

OCTOBER 12

Relaxing in your favorite spot with a warm drink and a good book is a terrific way to spend a lazy autumn afternoon or evening.

OCTOBER 13

Fall is the season to reap the rewards of all the hard work that went into preparing your garden, planting the seeds, and harvesting the fruits of your labor. If you have given the same devotion to your spiritual garden, those efforts as well will be richly rewarded.

OCTOBER 14

Some of the best ideas

come from simply being outdoors

and absorbing the world around you.

OctobeR 15

Fall brings families closer. Plan a meal with relatives or someone you love and enjoy the warmth of familiar smiles and good conversation.

OctobeR 16

"When one has weighed the sun in the balance, and measured the steps of the moon, and mapped out the seven heavens, there still remains oneself. Who can calculate the orbit of his own soul?"

De Profundis
—Oscar Wilde
born on this day in 1854

OCTOBER 17

Do not worry about the things you cannot change. Just as the seasons inevitably change, it is change that leads you forward into a better tomorrow.

OCTOBER 18

As the golden days of autumn go by, cooler weather makes the warmth of evening cuddles by a fireplace or candlelight feel even better. Make time for the simple things in life, as that is where you will often find life's most special moments.

OCTOBER 19

Always keep your thoughts in a positive place, and positive things will always happen.

OCTOBER 20

It's a lovely day to walk in the park, or if it's raining, stay warm inside and enjoy the view. Mother Nature shares her artistry every minute of every day. Don't get so busy that you forget to take time to look around and enjoy this wonderful gift.

OCTOBER 21

On this day in 1879, Thomas Edison changed the course of history. He didn't invent the incandescent light bulb, but he did create a new kind of bulb that burned longer and required less power, making it practical for everyday use. There's nothing new under the sun, as the saying goes, but what exists can always be improved. Think about one small but important change you can make to improve your life, and make that change today.

OCTOBER 22

Autumn inspires a mood of quiet peace and solitude that soon will be swept away by the cold winds of winter. Enjoy every moment of the season by living in the moment. Seize every opportunity for happiness and good fortune that comes your way.

OcToBeR 23

How boring life would be if the passage of time gave us only one season to enjoy, and worse, if that was the season you least enjoy. Fortunately, nature bestows four seasons, and as those seasons change, life goes on.

OcToBeR 24

Something about autumn inspires the urge to embrace and get closer to nature. Take time to stroll through the trees, find joy in raking leaves, visit a pumpkin patch, or go on an overnight camping trip. Positive memories are built on the positive and enjoyable things we do in daily life.

OCTOBER 25

Born on this day in 1881, Spanish painter Pablo Picasso was a creative genius who was always experimenting and pushing boundaries with his art. His life teaches us about the importance of pursuing one's passions. Despite challenges and setbacks, he remained dedicated to his art and continued to create and inspire. By following in Picasso's footsteps and embracing your own creativity, you can not only develop your own artistic skills but find greater meaning and fulfillment in life.

OCTOBER 26

Fall is an annual reminder from Mother Nature that starting over can lead to great things.

OCTOBER 27

"To waste, to destroy, our natural resources, to skin and exhaust the land instead of using it so as to increase its usefulness, will result in undermining in the days of our children the very prosperity which we ought by right to hand down to them amplified and developed."

—Theodore Roosevelt
born on this day in 1858

OCTOBER 28

Take a moment today to appreciate the deepening of autumn in all its glory. Notice the earthy colors, the rustle of falling leaves, the unmistakable smell of fall in the air. It's the season that ushers in winter's frosty slumber and the necessary change that allows rebirth in the spring.

OCTOBER 29

Have you ever tasted unsweetened pumpkin fresh scooped or from a can? It's quite bitter, and it takes a lot of sugar and spice to make a delicious slice of pumpkin pie. Sometimes you have to accept the bitter and make the most of it to enjoy the sweet.

OCTOBER 30

Many people love Halloween because it begins the countdown to the festivities of a bountiful Thanksgiving and a Christmas filled with good cheer. Now is the time to begin making plans for an unforgettably joyous holiday season.

OCTOBER 31

There's magic in the air tonight. Halloween is the one day of the year that you can put on a costume and be whoever you'd like—a superhero, arch-villain, a celebrity, ghost, or any other character you can imagine. Besides the fun of dressing up, this is a good day to create happy memories with family and friends, and there's lots of candy everywhere you turn.

NOVEMBER

NoVemBeR 1

The month of November is about nature's bounty and giving thanks. Take inventory of the positives in your life, and be grateful for where you are, what you have, and for those who love you.

NoVemBeR 2

The days grow shorter, bringing joy to those who love longer nights and shorter days. Nature teaches us that every cloud has a silver lining. Everything has its time and its season, in nature and in our lives.

NoVemBeR 3

November rains may seem colder and fall harder than the first showers of autumn, but they drive the last golden leaves from the trees. It's all part of the process.

NoVemBeR 4

November has a beauty all its own. Crimson sunsets, golden leaves, enchanting autumn breezes rustling through the trees. The fragrance of chimneys and holiday festivities awaken nostalgic memories. Nature's design brings joy in every season of the year.

NoVemBeR 5

There is no better time for a day trip to a scenic landmark or an afternoon hike with family or a friend to witness fall's splendor and write one more happy memory into your diary for this season of abundance and thanksgiving.

NoVemBeR 6

This month is represented by two birthstones that share the same rustic color but have diverse meanings in folklore. Topaz represents strength and intensity; it was associated with Ra, the Egyptian sun god. Citrine, also called "healing quartz," is thought to promote health, well- being, and serenity. The contrast symbolizes November's role as the gateway between the warm days of summer and cold winter nights to come as nature follows its eternal path from one season to the next.

NoVemBeR 7

Born on this day in 1867, Marie Curie was a pioneer in physics and chemistry, and the first woman to receive a Nobel Prize. Her research on radioactivity and her discovery of two new elements, polonium and radium, laid the foundation for advances in nuclear physics and medicine. Despite facing discrimination as a woman in science and the loss of her husband, she continued to persevere in her research and accomplishments. She once observed, "Life is not easy for any of us. But what of that? We must have perseverance and above all confidence in ourselves. We must believe that we are gifted for something and this thing must be attained." This quote reflects Curie's philosophy of believing in oneself and persevering to attain one's goals.

NoVemBeR 8

Togetherness and gratitude are two heartfelt qualities that will always make your house feel more like a home.

NoVEmBeR 9

Renowned astronomer author Carl Sagan was born on this day in 1934. He is known for many groundbreaking discoveries in astronomy, and he also worked to simplify complex scientific subjects through his published books, TV series, and other media. Sagan was a vocal advocate of critical thinking and skepticism, and he encouraged people to question their beliefs and evaluate evidence. His life and work have helped millions of people understand and appreciate the wonders of the universe.

NoVEmBeR 10

The brisk days of autumn bring opportunities to prepare for the winter and celebrate the good fortune and accomplishments you have experienced so far this year.

NoVemBeR 11

In this season of thanksgiving, consider all the positives that make a difference in your life, and thank the friends and others who contribute to your success or bring you happiness. Even a small gesture of appreciation will show hat you care.

NoVemBeR 12

Born on this day in 1815, Elizabeth Cody Stanton was an American writer and early leader of the women's rights movement in America. Her books passionately advocated for women to have the right to vote and other equal rights. In 1851, she met Susan B. Anthony, and the two became fierce opponents of slavery during the Civil War. Stanton is another shining example of how individuals can make a difference and have the power to change the world.

NoVEMBER 13

"To know what you prefer, instead of humbly saying amen to what the world tells you that you ought to prefer, is to have kept your soul alive."

An Inland Voyage
—Robert Louis Stevenson
born on this day in 1850

NoVEMBER 14

When you struggle with feeling down and believe you've done nothing to improve the world around you, think back to a time that you surprised someone and saw a spark of delight in their eyes. Think back to a time that you helped someone or made someone you care about feel loved or appreciated. Every positive act bears fruit. Your day-to-day presence has changed the world in ways you cannot begin to imagine.

NOVEMBER 15

Whether you keep a diary or journal, or write short stories or poetry for enjoyment, this is a special day—it's I Love to Write Day! Write something beautiful, inspired, or informative. Write something scary or funny. Write from your heart knowing that words have power—a special power that has shaped ideas and opinions, brought laughter and tears, and changed the course of history. If you love to write, set aside a few hours today and do what you love!

NOVEMBER 16

The world is nature's playground, and autumn is the bridge to a new year as nature's timeless cycle of rejuvenation follows its course. Learn to love nature and you will find beauty in every place you go and everywhere you look.

NoVemBeR 17

If you feel time is passing faster than it should and you are not accomplishing all that you'd like as autumn deepens, fill every day with productive activities that will bring you closer to your dreams.

NoVemBeR 18

Being happy never goes out of style. A smile is your best accessory, and a positive attitude is the best motivation to pave your road to success.

NoVemBeR 19

No matter how wonderful your spring and summer might have been, autumn brings the promise of good times with friends, a celebration of home and family, and a time to be thankful for the blessings in your life.

NoVemBeR 20

Only six weeks remain in this year. If you are going to fulfill all your new year's resolutions, now is the time for an enthusiastic push toward the finish line!

NoVEmBeR 21

When you are thankful for what you have, life will always give you more. When you flow with the tide, the Universe will always take you to the place where you are supposed to be.

NoVEmBeR 22

Born on this day in 1819, Mary Ann Evans adopted the pen name George Eliot because as a female author in the Victorian era, she faced prejudice and discrimination from publishers who refused to take women writers seriously. When she began publishing under "George Eliot" in the 1850s, many readers and critics praised her writing without realizing she was a woman. Eventually, her identity was revealed, and she became known as one of the most influential female writers of her time. Aptly, she wrote in her novel *Daniel Deronda* (1876): "It is never too late to be what you might have been." Often quoted as a personal growth affirmation, it suggests that no matter how old you are or what mistakes you've made in the past, you still have the power to change and become the person you have always wanted to be.

NoVemBeR 23

No matter what the weather might bring, acknowledge the golden bounty of nature all around and appreciate the beauty in this fall day. Move forward with a positive attitude and make today wonderful.

NoVemBeR 24

November is often viewed as a solemn, melancholy month. The trees are bare, the colors of spring and the warmth of summer have faded to a memory, and the first cold winds of winter have begun to gust. But this is the harvest month, a time of abundance and thanksgiving as nature completes its trek from fall to winter and begins writing the closing chapter of another year. If this has not been the best year of your life, you still have five weeks to make it so.

NoVemBeR 25

Today is White Ribbon Day, a global human rights effort inspired by the world's largest movement of men of all ages who seek to end violence against women and promote gender equality. Men are encouraged to wear a white ribbon on this day and for a week after to show their support for these goals. This is a perfect day to show a woman in your life how much you admire and respect her as a human being.

NoVemBeR 26

There's an invigorating, magical quality about late November evenings. The air is crisp, the fragrance of autumn wafts on the breeze, and stars twinkle brightly overhead. It's a wonderful time to take a mellow evening walk before winter's chill sets in. If you see a shooting star tonight, make a wish—November is an enchanted month that could make your fondest wish come true.

NoVemBeR 27

As autumn deepens, the days grow shorter, the nights longer, and the weather cooler, but November always brings a warm glow that brightens the rest of the year and lays the groundwork for a festive holiday season.

NoVemBeR 28

It's Red Planet Day, and on this day in 1964, Mariner 4 was launched to Mars. As the spacecraft completed its 228-day journey in July 1965, it sent back the first close-up photos of our closest planetary neighbor that has sparked man's imagination since the dawn of civilization. If you look up at the sky tonight, you might see Mars, a red pinpoint of light twinkling overhead.

NoVemBeR 29

Enjoy the autumn enchantment of golden meadows, leaves fluttering in the breeze, and the majestic limbs of once-green trees reaching skyward before winter's arrival conceals it all under a silent blanket of snow.

NoVemBeR 30

As November ends, one month remains in the year. It may be a busy month, filled with holiday cheer, family, and friends; but if you build on the positive mood, you can accomplish more than you imagine. Focus on your goals and move forward!

DECEMBER

DECEMBER 1

December derives from the Latin word Decembris, meaning "tenth month." In ancient Rome, it was a time of celebrations, most notably the Saturnalia, a joyous feast with gift-giving and revelry. Today, December continues to be a special time for spreading love, hope, and joy. How will you make your December one to remember?

DECEMBER 2

The winter season is a time to celebrate the power of the human spirit and our ability to persevere. Whether it's a personal accomplishment, helping someone in need during the holiday season, or taking the time to enjoy the simple things in life, make today a special day at this special time of the year.

DECEMBER 3

A good book, a warm beverage, and the flickering glow of candlelight might be the very definition of cozy during an early winter storm.

DECEMBER 4

If you live in the northern hemisphere, you likely have a few months of cold, stormy weather ahead. As the winter season approaches, look within to find the strength to weather the storms of life, and may the light and warmth of love always shine within your heart.

DECEMBER 5

Goals always seem unattainable just before opportunities arises for you to reach them.

DECEMBER 6

Today is more than just another date on the calendar. It's a new day that will bring new opportunities for growth and progress towards your goals. It's up to you to make the most of it.

DECEMBER 7

Sometimes what you consider a failure or mistake is simply the next thing that pushes you forward towards a slice of happiness that you were meant to discover.

DECEMBER 8

The winter season is all about perseverance. It makes you appreciate the blessings in your life, large and small, even more.

DECEMBER 9

Winter fashion provides the opportunity to express your personal style while staying warm. From stylish coats to cozy scarves, December is a great month to have fun with fashion and embrace the season.

DECEMBER 10

The comfort of warm drinks and hearty food is a source of solace as the days grow shorter. From sweet tasty cocoa to piping hot soup, there is nothing quite like the experience of enjoying these staples with someone you care about on a cold winter day.

DECEMBER 11

Sometimes one kind word or deed can illuminate an entire winter.

DECEMBER 12

Embrace the magic of the season. Make a special effort to spend time with family, friends, and loved ones. Reconnect with those you care about and celebrate the warmth of human interaction.

DECEMBER 13

Winter sparks magic in a creative mind. It is spring to the imagination.

DECEMBER 14

Don't let the snow stop you from enjoying the great outdoors. Skiing, sledding, throwing snowballs, making snow angels, or building a snowman are wonderful ways to enjoy the fresh air and rejuvenate your mind.

DECEMBER 15

If you think of winter as a celebration and not a season, no day will be a disappointment.

DECEMBER 16

It may be winter outside, but what season is it in your heart? Despite the cold and dreary weather, you have the power to cultivate warmth and positivity in yourself. Focus on what is thriving within, and you'll find a sense of joy and contentment that transcends the changing seasons of life.

DECEMBER 17

Bleak, gray days are a canvas waiting for warm thoughts and joy to paint an exquisite landscape.

DECEMBER 18

Winter holidays bring a sense of magic and wonder to the month of December. From the twinkling lights of Christmas trees and the aroma of fresh pine needles to the excitement of New Year's Eve, a festive atmosphere permeates the air. Enjoy the spirit of the season and share the light with family and friends.

DECEMBER 19

Some think of winter as a cold and desolate time, but if that's your view, broaden your perspective! Winter can be a time for adventure and exploration. From snowshoeing through the woods to building a snowman in the backyard, a sense of wonder comes from experiencing the world in a new way.

DECEMBER 20

Today is a golden opportunity for cozy chats by a crackling fire or spending quality time with family and loved ones. Whether you are playing a favorite board game or just lounging on the couch, there is something special about the togetherness this season brings.

DECEMBER 21

Today is the winter solstice in the northern hemisphere, the shortest day and longest night of the year. In ancient times, this was seen as a time of renewal. It was marked by lighting candles and decorating homes with evergreens, a symbol of enduring life in bleak winter. Hang an evergreen wreath on your door or light a candle to carry on the tradition and bring light into your own life on this frosty winter day.

DECEMBER 22

The holiday season is a time to give, not just receive. The act of giving is a powerful, transformative experience. By making the act of giving a regular part of your life, and by sharing your time and resources with those in need all year round, you can make the world a better place filled with kindness, generosity, and love.

DECEMBER 23

Find the joy in the journey, not just the destination. The holiday season is filled with anticipation for presents on Christmas Day and the revelry of New Year's Eve. But remember to find joy in the journey, in the simple moments and experiences that make the holiday season so special.

DECEMBER 24

May this magical night of Christmas Eve fill your heart with love and warmth, and may its light guide you towards a brighter tomorrow. Cherish this time with those you hold dear. Let the joy of the season surround you and stay with you throughout the coming year.

DECEMBER 25

Merry Christmas! This day marks a centuries-old tradition of people coming together to celebrate love, kindness, and generosity. It is a time to reflect on the blessings in your life, and to spread warmth and cheer around you. May the spirit of the holiday season fill your heart with happiness, hope, and peace.

DECEMBER 26

What better time than the day after Christmas to reflect on the simple things in life and find joy in the present moment. It's easy to get caught up in the hustle and bustle of the holidays, but today, take a break. Share the warmth of a hug from someone special, a beautiful sunrise or sunset, or a moment of peace and quiet.

DECEMBER 27

Winter can be a challenging season, and for some, it is a gray and gloomy time. But these cold, bleak days are also a testament to the human spirit. Celebrate your resilience and perseverance as you look back on what you've accomplished in the past year, and build on it to achieve even more in the new year ahead!

DECEMBER 28

December days spent with loved ones give this time of the year even more meaning. Memories made this holiday season will last a lifetime, so don't miss the opportunity to make some of the happiest moments of your life.

DECEMBER 29

The crisp, fresh air of December is invigorating. Find a few minutes to spend outdoors today. Breathe deeply and let the brisk air fill your lungs, clear your mind and rejuvenate your spirit.

DECEMBER 30

Setting positive and achievable goals for the new year is a great way to lay the foundation for happiness. Take the time to reflect on what you want to accomplish and what will make you truly happy. Then, make plans to turn those desires into reality.

DECEMBER 31

It's New Year's Eve! One chapter in your life is closing, and a new chapter begins tomorrow. As you turn to a new page in your life calendar, be prepared for new opportunities for success and the fulfillment of your dreams. Embrace each moment with courage, grace, and joy. Have a wonderful new year!

About the Author

Abby Leigh Hunter grew up near the cornfields of the Midwest, reading everything she could get her hands on. From her grandmother's stacks of *National Enquirer* and *The Star* to her mother's copies of *Reader's Digest* and *Cosmopolitan,* Abby developed a deep love of reading. She wanted to share and talk about the amazing things she read, which not surprisingly led to an interest in writing.

Abby spent her days in school reading the latest novels that caught her interest or writing poems and letters to friends instead of taking in her lessons. Her "too cool for school" attitude did not reflect well on her grades, but it did provide a creative outlet that would shape her adult life. Fascinated by the enduring tales the world's great authors of past and present could weave, she aspired to study them and one day write stories just as extraordinary. Her interest in classics led to an editor's role with an educational publisher, where her credits include academic editions of classics by Oscar Wilde and H.P. Lovecraft, with more to come.

Abby resides in a sleepy village on California's central coast with her husband (a lifelong writer/editor), their cat, and a yard full of blooming flowers and happy birds. She enjoys cliches, sunsets, long walks on the beach, and she will always love a good book.

Other Books by the Author:

The Picture of Dorian Gray (Academic Edition)
Oscar Wilde (Author); Abby Leigh Hunter (Editor)
Formats: e-book, paperback, hardcover

At the Mountains of Madness (Academic Edition)
H.P. Lovecraft (Author); Abby Leigh Hunter (Editor)
Formats: e-book, paperback, hardcover

The Whisperer in Darkness (Academic Edition)
H.P. Lovecraft (Author); Abby Leigh Hunter (Editor)
Formats: e-book, paperback, hardcover

The Dunwich Horror (Academic Edition)
H.P. Lovecraft (Author); Abby Leigh Hunter (Editor)
Formats: e-book, paperback, hardcover